STATES

ELISSA THOMPSON

DRAWING TEXAS'S

SIGHTS AND SYMBOLS

Enslow Publishing
101 W. 23rd Street
Suite 240
New York, NY 10011
USA

enslow.com

Published in 2019 by Enslow Publishing, LLC.
101 W. 23rd Street, Suite 240, New York, NY 10011

Library of Congress Cataloging-in-Publication Data

Names: Thompson, Elissa, author.
Title: Drawing Texas's sights and symbols / Elissa Thompson.
Description: New York : Enslow Publishing, 2019. | Series: Drawing our states|
Includes bibliographical references and index. | Audience: Grades 2-5.
Identifiers: LCCN 2018010812| ISBN 9781978503250 (library bound) |
ISBN 9781978504929 (pbk.) | ISBN 9781978504936 (6 pack)
Subjects: LCSH: Texas—In art—Juvenile literature. | Emblems in art—
Juvenile literature. | Drawing—Technique—Juvenile literature.
Classification: LCC NC825.T476 T49 2019 | DDC 741.09764—dc23
LC record available at https://lccn.loc.gov/2018010812

Printed in the United States of America

To Our Readers: We have done our best to make sure all websites in this book
were active and appropriate when we went to press. However, the author and
the publisher have no control over and assume no liability for the material
available on those websites or on any websites they may link to. Any comments
or suggestions can be sent by email to customerservice@enslow.com.

Photo Credits: Cover and p. 1 inset illustration and interior pages
instructional illustrations by Laura Murawski.

Cover, p. 1 atsurkan/Shutterstock.com (photo); p. 6 Ralph Crane/The LIFE
Picture Collection/Getty Images; p. 9 Dorothy Hood, Copper Signal, 1977,
oil on canvas, Collection of the Art Museum of South Texas, 2014.16.37;
p. 10 Creative Jen Designs/Shutterstock.com; p. 12 (top) BigAlBaloo/
Shutterstock.com; p. 12 (bottom) Heralder/Wikimedia Commons/File:
Reverse_of_the_Seal_of_Texas.svg/CC-BY-SA-3.0,2.5,2.0,1.0; p. 14 corund/
Shutterstock.com; p. 16 bcampbell65/Shutterstock.com; p. 18 Terry Vine/
J Patrick Lane/Blend Images/Getty Images; p. 20 Marcel van Kammen/
NiS/Minden Pictures/Getty Images; p. 22 Danita Delimont/Alamy Stock
Photo; p. 24 Steven Frame/Shutterstock.com; p. 26 Stephen Saks/Lonely
Planet Images/Getty Images; p. 28 LMPphoto/Shutterstock.com.

CONTENTS

WORDS TO KNOW

chaps Leather material worn over pants by cowboys to protect their legs.

Civil War The war fought between the northern and southern states of America from 1861 to 1865.

Confederate States States that fought for the South during the Civil War.

cupola A small structure built on a roof.

frontiersmen Men who live and work in an area that has not yet been settled.

industry A system of work or labor.

landmark An important building, structure, or place.

missions Places where religious leaders teach their religion.

ranch A large farm for raising horses, cattle, or sheep.

republic A form of government in which the authority belongs to the people.

Union The northern states that stayed loyal to the federal government during the Civil War.

WELCOME TO TEXAS

Native Americans called what is now Texas home long ago. They lived there before the sixteenth century, when Spanish explorers discovered the region. The first explorer to arrive, in 1519, was Alonso Álvarez de Pineda, a Spanish adventurer. After that, several other Spanish explorers visited the land, including Álvar Núñez Cabeza de Vaca in 1528 and Francisco Vásquez de Coronado in the 1540s. Spain ruled Texas from 1519 to 1685. France took over the territory from 1685 to 1690. Then the Spanish took back control of the land from 1690 to 1821.

In 1836, Texans fought a war for independence against Mexico. This war is famous for the Battle of the Alamo and the Battle of San Jacinto. The San Jacinto memorial monument is one of the tallest monument columns in the world. It is 570 feet (174 meters) high and stands as a symbol of freedom. After winning the war, Texas became an independent republic.

In 1845, Texas joined the Union and became part of the United States. In 1861, it left the Union and became part of the Confederate States. After the Civil War (1861–1865), Texas rejoined the United States.

Nearly five thousand farms and ranches in Texas have been owned by the same family for one hundred years or more!

The word "Texas" comes from the Native American word *tejas*, meaning "friendship." Friendship is Texas's state motto. Many of the people who live in Texas are Hispanic. Texas is the second most populated state in the country, and its nickname is the Lone Star State.

Texas has more acres of farmland than any other state. Main crops include wheat, pecans, melons, and potatoes. Cattle ranches make up two-thirds of the state. Cattle became important to the Texas economy in the mid-1800s, when trading and selling beef became a big industry.

Today Texas leads the nation in beef production. Other important products from Texas include oil, gas, cotton, and grain.

Texas has many great landmarks. Austin, the capital, is home to the nation's largest state capitol building. Fort Hood, near Killeen, is one of the largest military bases in the world. This base covers an area of 340 square miles (881 square kilometers)!

This book will teach you to draw some of Texas's sights and symbols. Each drawing starts with a simple step. From there, more steps are added.

You will need the following supplies to draw Texas's sights and symbols:

- A sketch pad
- An eraser
- A number 2 pencil
- A pencil sharpener

These are some of the shapes and drawing terms you need to know to draw Texas's sights and symbols:

- 3-D box
- Almond shape
- Horizontal line
- Oval
- Rectangle
- Shading
- Squiggle
- Teardrop
- Vertical line
- Wavy line

MEET DOROTHY HOOD

Dorothy Hood was born in Bryan, Texas, in 1919. She grew up in Houston and lived near the zoo. At night, she could hear the hyenas laugh! She went to the Rhode Island School of Design in the 1930s and modeled in New York to make money for art classes. When Hood graduated, she drove to Mexico City with some friends. She stayed in the country for twenty-two years, working alongside famous artists like Diego Rivera and Frida Kahlo. Famous poet Pablo Neruda wrote a poem about her paintings.

Hood married director and composer José María Velasco Maidana and they traveled all over the world for his work. When her husband became sick with Parkinson's disease, the couple moved back to Houston.

Hood continued painting, creating large pieces of artwork of the void of outer space, or the mind. Her paintings were abstract, and she used bright colors to make people feel. Many of her paintings were hung in new office buildings being built in downtown Houston.

Sometimes artists do not become popular until after they die. This happened with Hood. Not many people appreciated her art before she died from breast cancer in 2000 at the age of eighty-one. But now her

**Dorothy Hood, *Copper Signal*, 1977, oil on canvas,
Collection of the Art Museum of South Texas, 2014.16.37**

Even though she needed to make money, Hood did not always like to sell her paintings. Some pieces were too special or personal.

artwork has begun to get recognition. In 2016, the Art Museum of South Texas opened its biggest show ever on Hood's work. Her paintings have now been on display at the Museum of Modern Art in New York City and the Museum of Fine Art in Houston.

Miles and Miles of Wide-Open Spaces: Map of Texas

Texas is the second-largest US state. It is 801 miles (1,289 km) from north to south and 773 miles (1,244 km) from east to west, with an area of 267,277 square miles (692,244 sq km). The state is bordered by four states: New Mexico, Oklahoma, Arkansas, and

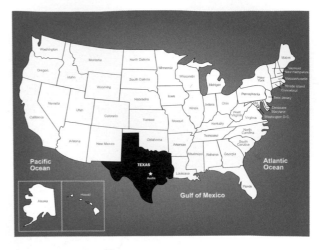

Louisiana. It is also bordered by the Gulf of Mexico. Texas is made up of plains, prairies, deserts, forests, lakes, and mountains. The Rio Grande forms Texas's border with Mexico. The state has ninety-one mountain ranges. Guadalupe Peak is the highest point at 8,749 feet (2,667 m).

1

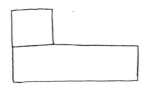

To draw Texas, begin by drawing a square. Next add a rectangle beneath the square.

2

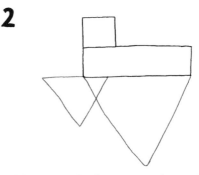

Add two upside-down triangles under the rectangle. Notice that they overlap. These shapes will be your guides as you draw the curvy borders of Texas.

3

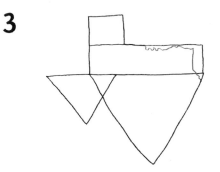

Carefully draw the border on the northeastern corner of the state.

4

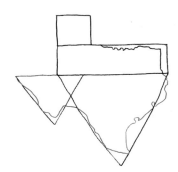

Continue drawing eastern and southern borders. Then draw the western border, using the triangles as guides. Erase extra lines.

5

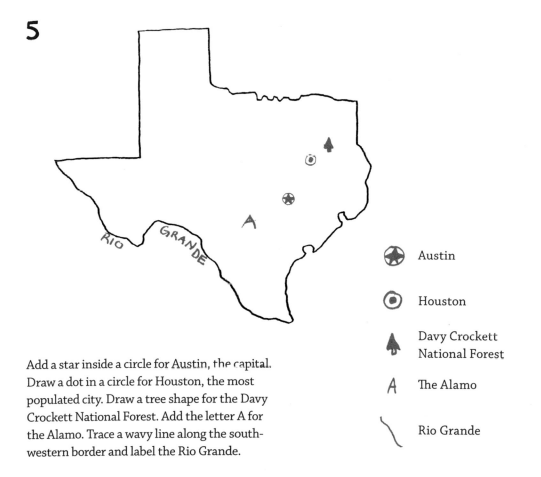

Add a star inside a circle for Austin, the capital. Draw a dot in a circle for Houston, the most populated city. Draw a tree shape for the Davy Crockett National Forest. Add the letter A for the Alamo. Trace a wavy line along the southwestern border and label the Rio Grande.

Austin

Houston

Davy Crockett National Forest

The Alamo

Rio Grande

Two Symbolic Sides: The State Seal

Texas's state seal was adopted in 1839. It has a single star on a light blue circle, surrounded by a wreath made of olive branches and oak leaves. In 1961, a design was added to the reverse side of the seal. This side of the seal is purely decorative. It depicts the Alamo, Vince's Bridge, and the Gonzales Cannon. This side of the seal also shows the six flags that have flown over Texas, the lone star, and two banners. The banner on the top reads "Remember the Alamo." The banner on the bottom reads "Texas One and Indivisible."

1

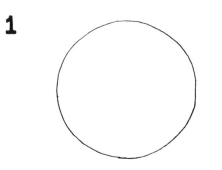

Let's draw the front of the seal. First draw a large circle.

2

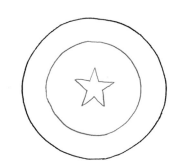

Add a smaller circle inside the first circle. Draw a star inside the smaller circle. If you need help drawing the star, look at the instructions on page 15.

3

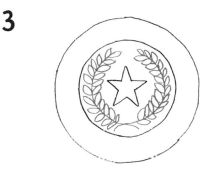

To draw the wreath, make two half circles for the branches. The leaves are almond shapes.

4

Print the words "THE STATE OF TEXAS" in the space between the two circles.

5

Shade the leaves. Finish your drawing by adding a line from each point and corner of the star into the star's center. Nice work!

The Lone Star: Texas's State Flag

Texas's state flag was adopted on January 24, 1839, while Texas was still a republic. When Texas became a state in 1845, it kept this design. The flag is red, white, and blue and has a single star. The red stands for bravery, the white for strength, and the blue for loyalty. The star represents Texas's nickname, the Lone Star State.

1

Texas's flag is easy to draw. Begin with a rectangle.

2

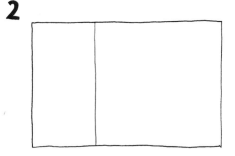

Next draw a vertical line on the left side of the flag.

3

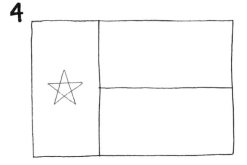

Add a horizontal line across the middle of the right side of the flag.

4

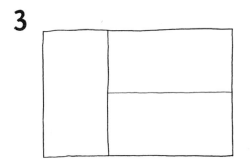

Draw a five-pointed star in the middle of the left side of the flag.

5

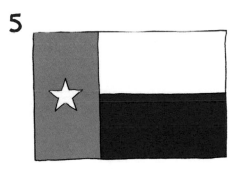

Erase the extra lines inside the star, shade your flag, and you're done!

State Flower Pride: The Bluebonnet

In 1901, the bluebonnet became Texas's state flower. The bluebonnet is named for its color and because it looks like a woman's bonnet. The Texas bluebonnet has clusters of blue flowers with white centers. Silky-haired leaves grow on its thick, spiky stem. The bluebonnet grows to be about 1½ feet (0.5 m) tall. This flower can be found throughout central and southern Texas. Texans take great pride in their state flower. They celebrate the bluebonnet with events like the Chappell Hill Bluebonnet Festival and with songs.

1

Begin making the bluebonnet by drawing a stem. Notice that the stem is wider on the bottom.

2

Draw a triangle for the basic shape of the bluebonnet. This will be your guide as you draw the individual flowers.

3

Next draw small almond shapes at the top of the stem.

4

Draw half circles for the first two buds near the top of the stem. The buds are flowers that have not yet bloomed. Add tiny stems coming out of the large stem.

5

Draw six more half-circle buds.

6

Next add a few buds that have opened into flowers.

7

At the base of the stem, draw leaves. The leaves are long almond shapes on a smaller stem. Erase extra lines.

8

To finish the drawing, add detail and shading. Don't forget the veins in the leaves.

A Sweet Symbol: The Pecan Tree

In 1919, the pecan tree (*Carya illinionensis*) was selected as the state tree of Texas. Pecan nuts, which grow on pecan trees, are one of Texas's most important crops. It is estimated that there are more than 600,000 acres (242,811 hectares) of pecan trees in Texas. These trees can live for more than 150 years. They can grow to be 150 feet (46 m) high and can be as wide as 3 feet (1 m) across. James Stephen Hogg, one governor of Texas, liked pecan trees so much he requested one be planted on his grave.

1

Begin by drawing a short tree trunk using slightly curved parallel lines.

2

Next draw four curved shapes. These will be the main branches of the pecan tree.

3

Add more branches.

4

Add more small branches. These branches should be made with thin lines.

5

Draw the fluffy outline of the leafy part of the tree using squiggly lines.

6

Shade the leafy part of the tree using more squiggly lines. Shade the trunk using darker straight lines to show the look of the bark.

Beautiful Singers: The Mockingbird

In 1927, the mockingbird (*Mimus polyglottos*) became Texas's state bird because of its beautiful singing voice. Mockingbirds can sing up to thirty different songs. It can imitate the songs of other birds that it hears and produce many other kinds of sounds, like a barking dog or squeaky hinges! The songbird lives in Texas year-round and is found in gardens, farms, deserts, and streamside thickets. It is medium-sized and gray and white, and it has a long tail.

1

Begin with an oval for the mockingbird's head.

2

Add another, larger oval for the body. Notice how this oval looks like an egg.

3

Draw a triangle for the beak.

4

Add a curved line that swoops across the body. At the end of the line, draw the mockingbird's leg and foot.

5

Add another leg and another foot coming from the body.

6

Draw a circle for the eye. You can also give the bird a perch on which to stand.

7

Soften the outline of the body. Notice that it looks like the tail feathers are behind the perch. Erase extra lines.

8

Add detail and shading. Pay attention to the spotty look of the feathers and the long shadow in front of the bird's eye.

The Wild West: Texas's Cowboys

When people think of Texas, many of them think of the state's Wild West history. The western United States became known as the Wild West during the late 1800s, when many people began moving to the region. Cowboys were frontiersmen who raised cattle. They developed the Wild West image of brave and independent men. They worked very hard and did not have easy lives. Cowboys dressed practically for their job, to protect themselves from weather and to be comfortable

while riding horses. They wore boots, a hat, and chaps over their pants. Cowgirls also contributed to Wild West lifestyle and history.

1

First draw a stick figure that will act as a guide. The stick figure should be standing like the cowboy in the picture.

2

Next add a triangle shape for the shoulders. Make the cowboy's arms by drawing curved lines on either side of the stick figure's arms.

3

Add the cowboy's legs. Use the same method that you used to make the cowboy's arms.

4

Next draw the cowboy's hat and boots. The shape of the boot is tricky, so look carefully at the picture.

5

Draw the cowboy's scarf and his vest by carefully following the picture.

6

Draw the shirt. Add cuffs and buttons to the shirt. Then draw the belt.

7

Add the spur to the boot. Draw the fringed chaps the cowboy wears. Add detail to the cowboy's face.

8

Shade your drawing. Great work!

Remember the Alamo: Texas History

One of Texas's most famous sites is the Alamo. This building is an old San Antonio mission used as a military post during Texas's fight for independence from Mexico. The Battle of the Alamo began on February

23, 1836. Mexican general Antonio López de Santa Anna surrounded the Alamo with between 1,800 and 6,000 men. There were only 189 men inside. Famous frontiersmen Davy Crockett and Jim Bowie were there. The battle lasted for twelve days. All 189 men inside died. As the men inside fought, they called out the now-famous saying, "Remember the Alamo."

1

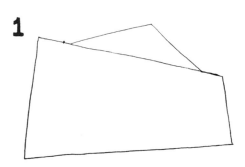

Begin by drawing a triangle on top of a quadrilateral. Notice that one end of the quadrilateral is smaller.

2

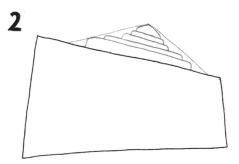

To draw the detailed roof, make four rectangles and a rounded triangle that are stacked like stairs.

3

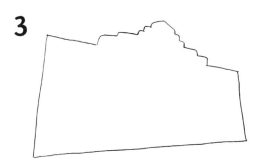

Erase extra lines.

4

Draw five rectangular windows and two arched windows.

5

Draw the door. Then make the column over the door.

6

Next draw another, taller column next to the door by layering rectangles on top of one another.

7

Add three more columns. Connect them with lines that go across the tops of the columns.

8

Finish by shading your drawing. To create the rough look of the building, use wavy lines.

Look to the Stars: The Johnson Space Center

The Manned Spacecraft Center opened in 1963 in Houston, Texas. In 1973, the center was officially renamed the Johnson Space Center. It is part of the National Aeronautics and Space Administration (NASA). More than fif-teen thousand engineers,  scientists, astronauts, and support members work there. This center has exhibits on space flight and astronauts. You can visit and see a Gemini spacecraft, a Mercury mission capsule, and an Apollo 17 com-mand module there. Visitors can try on a space helmet, hold moon rocks, and use computers to see how astronauts live and work in space.

1 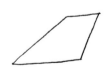 **2**

Start by drawing the tail of the spacecraft. It is made with two horizontal lines and two diagonal lines.

Next draw the body of the spacecraft using curved lines.

3

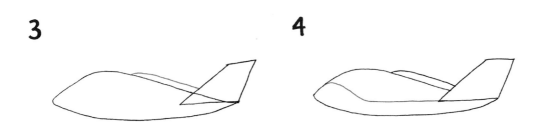

Draw a bump on the top of the spacecraft. Everything on your spaceship needs to be smooth so it can move through the air quickly.

4

Use a curved line to divide the spacecraft into two sections.

5

Erase extra lines.

6

Add the words "NASA" and "United States" and an American flag to the side of the spacecraft.

7

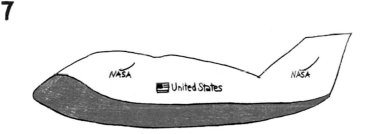

Shade the belly of the ship. Now your X-38 spacecraft is ready to bring people back from space!

A Fitting Monument: Texas's Capitol

Texas is the second largest state in the country—but it has the largest state capitol building in the nation! The building is more than 300 feet (91 m) tall and 500 feet (152 m) long. It is made of pink granite and is located in Texas's state capital, Austin. Architect E. E. Myers designed the building, which was completed on December 8, 1888. The inside of the building has elaborate woodwork. A statue of the Goddess of Liberty stands on top of the capitol's dome as a symbol of freedom.

1

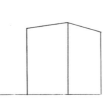

Begin by drawing a horizontal line across the bottom of the page. Add the first section of the building. It is made with three vertical lines connected at the top with two diagonal lines.

2

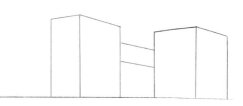

Draw a similar shape to the left. Connect the two shapes with diagonal lines.

3

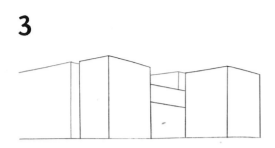

Add the two thin sections of the capitol. These are both made by drawing a vertical line and two slanted lines.

4

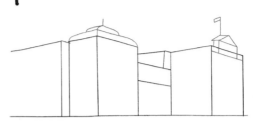

Next draw the rounded roofs of the section on the left. Add the house shape and flag on the section on the right.

5

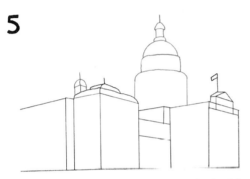

Add the tower on the left side of the building. Draw the outline of the dome. Notice that the dome has three sections. The shape on the top of the dome is called a cupola. The cupola also has three sections.

6

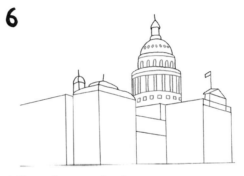

Add windows to the dome.

7

Add windows to the lower parts of the building. Draw a tall arch for the doorway on the right.

8

Now draw trees in front of the building. Shade and add detail to your drawing.

TEXAS STATE FACTS

Statehood • December 29, 1845, the 28th state
Area • 267,277 square miles (692,244 sq km)
Population • 28,304,596
Capital • Austin, population, 947,890
Most Populated City • Houston, population, 2,303,482
Industries • Chemical products, petroleum and natural gas,
    machinery, mining
Agriculture • Cattle, cotton, dairy products, corn, peanuts, pecans,
    rice, wheat
Flower • Bluebonnet
Tree • Pecan
Bird • Mockingbird
Nickname • The Lone Star State
Motto • Friendship
Song • "Texas Our Texas"
Gemstone • Blue topaz

LEARN MORE

Books

Gregory, Josh. *Texas*. New York, NY: Scholastic, 2018.

Hale, Nathan. *Alamo All Stars*. New York, NY: Amulet Books, 2016.

Smith, Maximilian. *The History of Juneteenth*. New York, NY: Gareth Stevens Publishing, 2016.

Websites

Kids' House: Texas House of Representatives

kids.house.state.tx.us

Learn all about Texas state government with this interactive website.

Texas Independence

txindependence.org

This website has many features on Texas's fight for independence from Mexico, including a timeline, biographies, and games.

INDEX